PERFORMANCE EDITIONS

RACHMANINOFF

PRELUDES
Opus 3 and Opus 23

Edited and Recorded by Alexandre Dossin

T0071694

To access companion recorded performances online, visit:
www.halleonard.com/mylibrary

Enter Code
2357-9247-8130-5677

On the cover:
Stormy Sea (1906)
by Wassily Kandinsky
(1866–1944)

ISBN: 978-1-4584-0305-6

G. SCHIRMER, *Inc.*

DISTRIBUTED BY
HAL•LEONARD®

www.halleonard.com

Contact us:
Hal Leonard
7777 West Bluemound Road
Milwaukee, WI 53213
Email: info@halleonard.com

In Europe, contact:
Hal Leonard Europe Limited
42 Wigmore Street
Marylebone, London, W1U 2RN
Email: info@halleonardeurope.com

In Australia, contact:
Hal Leonard Australia Pty. Ltd.
4 Lentara Court
Cheltenham, Victoria, 3192 Australia
Email: info@halleonard.com.au

CONTENTS

The price of this publication includes access to companion recorded performances online, for download or streaming, using the unique code found on the title page. Visit **www.halleonard.com/mylibrary** and enter the access code.

HISTORICAL NOTES

SERGEI RACHMANINOFF (1873–1943)

Sergei Rachmaninoff was born on one of his grandparents' estates in Oneg, a region of Novgorod in the northwestern part of Russia. [1] Sergei's parents were wealthy landowners and provided him with a comfortable childhood for the first ten years of his life. Financial problems arose due to his father's poor handling of the family affairs which generated a crisis that ended not only in the parents' divorce, but also in a radical change in life style with Sergei and his mother moving to a small flat in Saint Petersburg.

Sergei displayed natural talent for the piano at an early age and his mother arranged for a graduate student at the Saint Petersburg Conservatory to teach him in their home. Rachmaninoff did not do well at the conservatory and, upon the suggestion of his cousin Alexander Siloti, moved to Moscow in 1886, joining the piano studio of Nikolai Zverev. Siloti was already a renowned pianist, having just returned from several years in Weimar, where he studied under Franz Liszt.

Photo credit: George Grantham Bain collection @ wikipedia.com

Nikolai Zverev was a famous pedagogue in Moscow, teaching privately and at the junior division of the Moscow Conservatory. He also kept up to three talented piano students as boarders tuition free. Rachmaninoff joined Matvei Pressman and Leonid Maximov in this capacity. In this new environment, Rachmaninoff spent hours practicing piano and studied other musical subjects.

In 1888, at age 16, Sergei was admitted in the conservatory's senior department as a student of Siloti. Three years later, disagreements between Vladimir Safonov, the powerful new director of the Conservatory, and Alexander Siloti resulted in Siloti's resignation from his post at the Moscow Conservatory. Not interested in changing piano teachers for his last year of study, Rachmaninoff was allowed to finish his studies one year earlier than normal.

Many successful compositions appeared during the early 1890s, including the Prelude in C-sharp minor. In 1897, however, damning reviews of his first symphony drove Rachmaninoff to the edge of depression. For a few years he could not find inspiration to compose and started a conducting career. After consultations with Dr. Nikolai Dahl in psychotherapy sessions that may have involved hypnotic suggestion, Sergei returned to composition with full force and immediately composed several works that became worldwide successes. The list includes the famous Piano Concerto in C minor, one of the most-often performed and recorded concertos in the piano repertoire.

In 1902, Rachmaninoff married his cousin Natalya Satina, and in 1903 their first daughter, Irina, was born. The family was complete in 1907 with the birth of their youngest daughter Tatiana.

The events that culminated in the 1917 revolution in Russia forced Rachmaninoff to emigrate with his young family. Needing to find ways to support his family outside his homeland, Rachmaninoff turned to piano performance as his main source of income. From that period until his death in 1943 he was a constant presence as a celebrated soloist with the best orchestras and in the most important concert venues in Europe and the United States.

Most of his piano works were composed before he left Russia. His only concerto composed after 1917 (No. 4 in G minor, Op. 40) was never received with the same enthusiasm as the previous two concertos (C minor and D minor), and the other two major piano works (*Variations on a Theme by Corelli*, Op. 42 and *Rhapsody on a Theme of Paganini*, Op. 43) are variations on foreign themes. It is almost as if Russia and piano music were so interconnected in his nature that away from his homeland Rachmaninoff could not find the inspiration to compose piano masterworks on his own themes. He never returned to his beloved Russia.

PERFORMANCE NOTES

Rachmaninoff's Piano Music

Fingering

Fingerings are largely editorial and have in mind a medium-sized hand. Some adjustments may be needed for smaller hands. As a rule, fingerings were carefully chosen to convey the phrasing and articulation, not simply for comfort. Two numbers connected by a hyphen represent a slide between black and white keys; two numbers connected by a slur represent finger substitution. In some cases, an optional fingering is shown under or above in parenthesis. When available, Rachmaninoff's own fingerings are shown in italics. Alternate division of notes between hands is indicated by finger brackets.

Pedaling

It is extremely difficult to notate pedaling in an effective way, especially when dealing with such complex pianistic textures as Rachmaninoff's. Good pedaling depends on many variables (quality of the instrument, performer's touch, how far the pedal is pressed, specific acoustics, etc.), that any effort becomes almost pointless, since the performer will need to make the final decisions using his or her musical abilities and sensibilities. Therefore, pedal indications are omitted with the exception of Rachmaninoff's own pedal marking in a few places. It is assumed that performers working on these pieces will have the necessary skills for a successful choice of pedaling. Use the pedal in such a way so the textures are always clear and not compromised by excessive blurring.

Metronome Markings

Metronome markings are original. Rachmaninoff typically did not provide metronome markings for his works; however, the Preludes, Op. 23 are among the few works he did make specific suggestions. His markings are meant only as basic indications of tempo; the music requires a refined flexibility and an organic rubato. In two of the preludes, the metronome indications are very fast and would require utmost virtuosity to project the musical ideas with the necessary clarity at the

suggested tempo (see notes for the A-flat Major and E-flat minor preludes). A review of several recordings shows that in those two particular cases performers do not adhere to Rachmaninoff's original markings. Unfortunately Rachmaninoff did not record those preludes.

Dynamics and Articulation

Dynamics and articulations are Rachmaninoff's. Considered a very thorough proof-reader, Rachmaninoff was very consistent in his writing. There were virtually no inconsistencies in the articulation and phrase markings in the first editions, editions based on autographs, and modern editions. See the notes below on the individual pieces for a discussion on the minor discrepancies between editions.

Rachmaninoff's Preludes

The collection of 24 piano preludes, one in every major and minor key, was not composed at once. The earliest work from this group is the one that has became almost synonymous with Rachmaninoff's name: the celebrated Prelude in C-sharp minor, Op. 3, No. 2, dedicated to his composition teacher, Anton Arensky. Later came ten preludes published as opus 23, composed from 1901–1903. This set is dedicated to his cousin, celebrated pianist Alexander Siloti. Siloti was instrumental not only in Rachmaninoff's piano instruction (first by placing him under Zverev and then as teacher at the Moscow Conservatory) but also in his private life, providing generous financial support to the struggling young composer. Siloti was the first pianist to perform the complete set of the opus 23 preludes in 1904. [2]

In 1910, fresh after his successful tour and premiere of his third piano concerto in the United States, Rachmaninoff completed the final thirteen preludes, published as opus 32. It is assumed that Rachmaninoff came up with the idea of composing a cycle of 24 preludes in all keys mirroring Chopin's set of Preludes, Op. 28, the classic example of this genre, and Scriabin's opus

11 which were very well-received by critics and audiences. It was only natural for Rachmaninoff to contribute to this tradition. The thirteen preludes of opus 32 covered all remaining keys left out of the previous, and returned to the same tonic (D-flat/C-sharp) of the first prelude, ending the set with a broad, cyclical arch.

Notes on the Individual Pieces

Prelude in C-sharp minor, Op. 3, No. 2

One of the pieces included in *Morceaux de fantaisie*, this prelude is certainly the most famous solo piano work written by Rachmaninoff, and a great example of how simplicity generates great works of art. This short piece, only 61 measures long, has many elements of Rachmaninoff's signature style: big chordal textures and huge dynamic contrasts coupled with virtuosic sections and a big culmination. The prelude has become as widely recognized by the piano-loving audiences as Mozart's Turkish March and Beethoven's Für Elise and has made Rachmaninoff a household name.

The musical material of this prelude is very succinct with short motives and a recurrent rhythmic figure. What makes it stand out is Rachmaninoff's brilliant textural creativity. Nicknamed by publishers "The Bells of Moscow," this piece has a resonant bass throughout, and displays a very appealing start, with the descending motive (A–G-sharp–C-sharp) played *fortissimo*. This motive returns repeatedly in the A sections and is the "signature" of the celebrated work. Rachmaninoff himself became tired of it; he was constantly asked to perform it as an encore whenever he concertized.

This is the only prelude for which we have three Rachmaninoff recordings available. The recordings are very helpful when analyzing some discrepancies in the available editions. An important example is found in measures 5 and 48. Many editions include natural signs before the D's in the left hand. This issue has been thoroughly investigated by Hui-Ying Liu-Tawaststjerna. After examining numerous printed editions, she concluded that in 36 editions

> "(…) either a sharp or a natural has been added to the D's. No explanation has been found for why Gutheil's first print (Print A) contains the natural signs. Since Rachmaninoff himself played D-sharps in his recordings—the way it is indicated in his autograph—the D-naturals must be

considered engraver's mistakes. To correct this error, Gutheil presumably replaced all the naturals with sharps in the subsequent prints." [3]

Another example is found in measures 6 and 49. In the original manuscript, there are G-sharp Major chords in the beginning of the measures. However, all editions omit the sharp signs. According to Dr. Tawaststjerna,

> "it is assumed here therefore that Rachmaninoff gave his consent, before the first edition was printed, to replace all the G-sharp Major chords with G-sharp minor ones, an assumption that seems to be confirmed by Rachmaninoff's recorded performances of this Prelude." [4]

The performer of this prelude will be confronted with several challenges: textural control in the first section, virtuosic passages in the middle section, and heavy chords played by both hands, using the entire keyboard range in the recapitulation of the main section.

Prelude in F-sharp minor, Op. 23, No. 1

The set of ten preludes begins with an ominous, dark piece. The main challenge to the performer is the polyphonic texture, requiring advanced control of touch, dynamics, and articulation. The musical language—highly chromatic and with scant melodic material—will return in Rachmaninoff's work more than once. One clear example is from variation XVII of *Rhapsody on a Theme of Paganini* for piano and orchestra, composed in 1934. Pedal should be used with great care, keeping the three main textural layers well defined. Use arm weight to project the long melodic notes and a distinction between finger and wrist weight in the left-hand accompaniment figure. The left-hand chords in measures 39–41 require a very large hand with a span of an octave between fingers 5 and 2. Instead of rolling the chords, I suggest omitting the second F-sharp from the bottom. There are still three F-sharps in the chord, so the difference in sound will be minimal with no loss for the final, tonic quality of the chords.

Prelude in B-flat Major, Op. 23, No. 2

The contrast could not be bigger. The prelude begins with "all stops pulled" and a rich sound, exploring a wide range of the keyboard. It is a tour de force for the left hand with textures that are typical in Rachmaninoff's music: a mix of scales and arpeggios encompassing several octaves in a few beats. The "bell" sound is very obvious in this piece, and one of the main challenges that confront the player is how to maintain a strong sound (*ff, sempre marcato*) without forcing it. The middle section begins in measure 8 with a two-measure weakening of the sound. The entrance of a powerful tenor line at the end of measure 19 brings some variety to the texture. The bells in the right hand give way to a melody which is full of Russian melancholy. Rachmaninoff's use of the keyboard proves once more his mastery of the instrument. Three distinct layers permeate this section, challenging the pianist to keep perfect control of touch throughout. After the "soft culmination" in measure 27, the performer is confronted with a rhythmically complex section, requiring independence of hands. One should be able to listen to each hand as if coming from different stereophonic speakers instead of trying to synchronize one to the other. After several measures using imitation technique, the listener is prepared for the triumphant return of the main section.

The return of the A section is an exact repeat of the first 17 measures and the coda begins in measure 54. It has a scintillating, shimmering quality, with high-register 32nd notes in the right hand that brings the piece to a brilliant end in a bravura display of octaves.

Prelude in D minor, Op. 23, No. 3

This prelude displays a different style from the typical Rachmaninoff texture, full of cascades of notes. Instead, we are transported to an almost baroque feeling with a dance-like, chordal texture marked *Tempo di minuetto* by Rachmaninoff. This prelude is more understated when compared to the previous prelude; a *fortissimo* is briefly reached in m. 35, but does not last for very long. The challenge of the prelude is, in a way, the opposite of the previous prelude. The pianist here is challenged to keep a moderate sound for a long time while maintaining the distinction between the layers. The texture is at times polyphonic (mm. 18–20 and mm. 22–28), and some intervals require a large span for the left hand (m. 31). The energetic motive that appears at the beginning (the 32nd-note triplets in the left hand of measures 2 and 4) is a very important element in the musical discourse of this small but powerful piece. The motive contrasts with the static eighth-note chords of the first measure on three levels: dynamic, rhythmic and melodic. This motive returns several times and can also be recognized

in an augmented form in measures 18 and 22 in the left hand. Motivic unity is very clear in this prelude. Notice how the culminating measures (mm. 35–45) repeat over and over the melodic material from the first theme in diminution, while immediately contrasting it with the motive in 32nd-note triplets. The coda, beginning in measure 55, requires the use of the sostenuto pedal to sustain the tonic note for several measures while maintaining clarity in the remaining layers.

Prelude in D Major, Op. 23, No. 4

Long melodic material, well-delineated accompaniment surrounding the melody, and rich harmonies are the winning ingredients of this expressive masterpiece. Even though it is possible to use the original hand distribution, we suggest fingering and strategic placement of hand positions based on a very smooth, *cantabile* right hand. Of course this solution creates other challenges, such as the need to voice evenly the accompaniment material between hands. The repeat of the main theme beginning in measure 19 separates the texture in three clear layers: the melodic in the middle, surrounded by a counter melody in the top and the arpeggiated accompaniment in the left hand. In the middle section, long melodic lines create waves that reach the softest point (m. 43) before building to the climax in measure 51 which leads to the return of the A section in yet one more textural variation. The theme is now presented in chords, with a syncopated counter melody on the weak part of the beat a sixth above the theme. Rachmaninoff believed in the importance of finding a culminating point in each piece (*totchka* in Russian) for a successful performance. In this prelude, one could argue that there are two such points, one soft (*pp*, m. 43), and one loud (m. 51). For a successful performance, both places should be brought out in a special way. A tasteful use of *rubato* will be necessary throughout.

Prelude in G minor, Op. 23, No. 5

After the Prelude in C-sharp minor, Op. 3, No. 2, the G-minor prelude is the most famous. The reasons are clear: exciting rhythm, rich textures, virtuosic chordal sections, brilliant octaves, and a middle section that could be written only by Rachmaninoff. The performer of this prelude will be confronted with numerous pianistic challenges: repeated chords in various dynamic levels, complex articulation (*staccato* in one hand with *legato* in the other in places like measures 7 and 8), and several other difficulties. The middle section, rich in melodic and harmonic content, requires a good control of *legato* in the large chords of the right hand, and fluent left-hand arpeggios. As usual in Rachmaninoff's piano music, the amount of notes to be played is by itself a challenge; however, one should avoid a performance that only displays the many notes, and should instead follow the original slurs that show clearly how many notes should be played under one gesture.

This is one of the preludes for which we have an original Rachmaninoff recording. Interestingly enough, he adds two extra notes at the end of the prelude. Those notes are not found in the autograph nor in the editions printed during his lifetime. This is the first prelude of this set Rachmaninoff wrote, composed in 1901.

Prelude in E-flat Major, Op. 23, No. 6

This Prelude is a great example of Rachmaninoff's masterly writing for the left hand. According to Julian Haylock, this prelude was composed on the day his first daughter, Irina, was born.[5] It is a beautiful, waving melody that at the same time complements wonderfully the right-hand melodic/harmonic texture. In a fascinating way, this prelude inverts the normal texture with a chordal right hand accompanied by a melodic left hand. Similarly to No. 4, this short masterpiece has two clear culminating points: a loud one (*f*, m. 19) and a soft one (*pp*, m. 28). Both should be carefully prepared, for without a successful execution of these passages, the piece looses its effect. The rather detailed and specific fingering offered is geared towards a fluent and expressive rendition of the left-hand melody.

Prelude in C minor, Op. 23, No. 7

Bells return with full force in this virtuosic prelude. Composed in the same key as the famous Piano Concerto No. 2, the prelude displays non-stop motion, *moto perpetuo*, in sixteenth notes. The texture is cleverly built, resulting in a clear "three-hands effect." The fast tempo required by Rachmaninoff (MM = 80 for the half-note) will only work with a clear definition between sixteenth notes, quarter notes, and also half notes marked in the score. These notes delineate hidden motives that are also present in the sixteenth notes. The pianist needs to access the reverberation of the instrument when choosing the appropriate

touch. Pedal should be generously used, but a thick sound will create a blurry texture.

Prelude in A-flat Major, Op. 23, No. 8

This is another prelude requiring extreme dexterity in the right hand. Rachmaninoff's metronome marking (MM = 108 for the half note), with a texture of non-stop sixteenth notes throughout, is almost impossible to reach. At MM = 216 for each quarter note, this would require an astounding rate of about 12 notes per second! Most recordings do not reach that speed, going to a maximum of MM = 180 for the quarter note (still a remarkable feat). In order to achieve the fast tempo required, even if under Rachmaninoff's original tempo, one needs to differentiate clearly between the quarter notes (marked with stems down) and the accompanying sixteenth notes. They should be played in the same gesture as the quarter notes; a supple wrist will do the trick. Special textural control will be necessary in the section from measure 32 until measure 42. The dynamic markings (mostly *pp*) coupled with the proximity between the layers require a very careful and light touch. The long notes in the left hand cannot be held with the finger alone since the right hand also uses the same keys. The only solution is a very refined use of the pedal.

Prelude in E-flat minor, Op. 23, No. 9

Definitely the hardest in this set, this reminds one of Liszt's famous "Feux-Folets" from the *Transcendental Études*, and to a less extent, Schumann's Toccata, Op. 7. Unlike Liszt, though, Rachmaninoff uses fast double notes throughout the piece in a real *perpetuum mobile* tour de force. Here again, the metronome marking is almost impossible to achieve. Of all recordings researched, most pianists stay under the required MM = 152 for the quarter note. Of course, all recordings use some *rubato*, but the average tempo in those recordings varies from MM = 120–140. Unfortunately, Rachmaninoff did not record this prelude. It is interesting to note that Liszt's metronome marking is MM = 120–126 for the eighth-note ("Feux-Folets" is written in 2/4, with thirty-second notes instead of sixteenth notes). Even at that speed, "Feux-Folets" is considered one of the hardest works in the piano repertoire. The overall dynamic of Rachmaninoff's Prelude in E-flat minor is *p–pp*, with a few outbursts of *f* and *mf*. A light legato touch with the fingers very close to the key (not really allowing the keys to go all the way up), will help with the speed and texture.

Be prepared for hours and hours of practice to be culminated in only 2 minutes of performance.

Prelude in G-flat Major, Op. 23, No. 10

The opus 23 group of Preludes ends softly with this inspired, short piece. After the difficult texture found in the Prelude in E-flat minor, this one may seem at first glance technically easy. In fact, the thick texture of the last section (beginning in m. 47) is the only moment when the performer is asked to display some technical expertise. However, musical challenges abound: long melodic notes in the left hand are accompanied by melodic-like chords in the right hand. Not surprisingly, this prelude exists in a version for cello and piano. Starting in measure 9, the texture is expanded to include a conversation between left and right hands, accompanied by chords in the middle register. It is very important to give each layer its own color, presenting all layers with great clarity. Rachmaninoff's recording of this prelude is very expressive and free, with a decisive *accelerando* and *crescendo* in the middle section (mm. 19–30), and a refined control of layers. He adds a B-flat in the right hand (m. 55), not found in any of the available editions. Rachmaninoff also ends the prelude quietly, contrary to most editions, which have a *f* above the last two chords. Only the 2006 Russian Music Publishing/Bärenreiter edition indicates *p* for these chords.

Notes:

[1] There has been confusion about Rachmaninoff's real birthplace. He always mentioned Oneg as his birthplace, but some scholars believe he was born at Semyonovo, and moved to Oneg because of his father's unfortunate financial decisions.

[2] Several sources indicate February 10, 1903 as the first complete performance of opus 23. However, according to Apetian (*Rachmaninoff: Letters*, p. 222), only three preludes were performed by the composer on that day: Prelude in F-sharp minor, B-flat Major, and G minor. Siloti's performance of opus 23, according to Antipov, was on November 13, 1904, in Saint Petersburg.

[3] Tawaststjerna, p. 40.

[4] ibid., p. 41.

[5] "A baby daughter, Irina, was born on May 14, in response to which Rachmaninov sat down the very same day and composed his *E flat Major Prelude* (no. 6), a microcosm of wide-eyed innocence and blissful contentment." Haylock, p. 33.

Editions Consulted:

Prelude, Op. 3, No. 2

Rachmaninoff, Sergei. *Prelude in C-sharp minor, Op. 3, No. 2*. London: Boosey & Hawkes, 1893.

Rachmaninoff, Sergei. *Prelude in C-sharp minor, Op. 3, No. 2*. Edited by Louis Oesterle. New York: G. Schirmer, Inc., 1898 (renewed, 1925).

Rachmaninoff, Sergei. *Prelude in C-sharp minor, Op. 3, No. 2*. Milan: Casa Ricordi, 1936.

Rachmaninoff, Sergei. *Prelude in C-sharp minor, Op. 3, No. 2*. Mainz, Germany: Schott Music, 1961.

Rachmaninoff, Sergei. *Prelude in C-sharp minor, Op. 3, No. 2: Facsimile*. Moscow: State Publishers, Muzika, 1977.

Rachmaninoff, Sergei. *Prelude in C-sharp minor, Op. 3, No. 2*. Budapest, Hungary: Editio Musica Budapest, 2006.

Prelude, Op. 3, No. 2 as part of *Fantasy Pieces*, Op. 3

Rachmaninoff, Sergei. *Fantasy Pieces, Op. 3*. Edited by Murray Baylor. Van Nuys, California: Alfred Music Publishing, 1986.

Rachmaninoff, Sergei. *Fantasy Pieces, Op. 3*. Boca Raton, Florida: Master Music Publications, 1992.

Prelude, Op. 23, No. 5

Rachmaninoff, Sergei. *Prelude in G minor, Op. 23, No. 5*. Edited by Louis Oesterle. New York: G. Schirmer, Inc., 1904.

Rachmaninoff, Sergei. *Prelude in G minor, Op. 23, No. 5*. London: Boosey & Hawkes, 1904.

Rachmaninoff, Sergei. *Prelude in G minor, Op. 23, No. 5*. Edited by Murray Baylor. Van Nuys, California: Alfred Music Publishing, 1987.

Preludes, Op. 23

Rachmaninoff, Sergei. *Preludes Op. 23*. Moscow: A. Gutheil, 1904.

Rachmaninoff, Sergei. *Preludes Op. 23*. New York: G. Schirmer, Inc., 1904.

Rachmaninoff, Sergei. *Preludes Op. 23*. Moscow: Muzgiz, ca. 1948.

Rachmaninoff, Sergei. *Preludes Op. 23*. Edited by Murray Baylor. Van Nuys, California: Alfred Music Publishing, 1987.

Rachmaninoff, Sergei. *Preludes Op. 23*. Moscow: "Kristina" Publishing House, 1992.

Rachmaninoff, Sergei. *Preludes Op. 23*. Saint Petersburg: "Kompozitor" Publishing House, 1993.

Complete Preludes, Op. 3, No. 2; Op. 23; and Op. 32

Rachmaninoff, Sergei. *Preludes Op. 3 No. 2, Op. 23 and Op. 32*. Van Nuys, California: Alfred Music Publishing, 1988.

Rachmaninoff, Sergei. *Preludes Op. 3 No. 2, Op. 23 and Op. 32*. Edited by Robert Threlfall. London: Boosey & Hawkes, 1992.

Rachmaninoff, Sergei. *Preludes Op. 3 No. 2, Op. 23 and Op. 32*. New York: G. Schirmer, Inc., 1994.

Rachmaninoff, Sergei. *Preludes Op. 3 No. 2, Op. 23 and Op. 32*. Moscow: Russian Music Publishing/ Bärenreiter, 2006.

Bibliography:

Scott, Michael. *Rachmaninoff.* Stroud, Gloucestershire: The History Press Ltd., 2008.

Lui-Tawaststjerna, Hui-Ying. *Rachmaninoff's Prelude in C-sharp minor, Op. 3, No 2: The Composer's Notation and His Three Interpretations.* Helsinki: Sibelius Academy, 2004.

Haylock, Julian. *Sergei Rachmaninov: An Essential Guide to His Life and Works.* London: Pavilion Books 1997.

Norris, Geoffrey. *Rakhmaninov.* London: J. M. Dent & Sons Ltd, 1976.

Bertensson, Sergei, and Jay Leyda. *Sergei Rachmaninoff: A Lifetime in Music.* New York: New York University Press, 1956.

Apetian, Zarui, editor. *S.V. Rachmaninoff: Pis'ma.* Moscow: State Musical Publisher, 1955.

Seroff, Victor I. *Rachmaninoff.* New York: Books for Libraries Press, 1950.

Audio Credits:

Lance Miller, Recording Engineer

Alexandre Dossin, Producer and Pianist

Recorded at Beall Concert Hall, University of Oregon School of Music and Dance

PRELUDES

Opus 3 and Opus 23

à Monsieur A. Arensky

Prelude in C-sharp Minor

from *Morceaux de fantaisie*

Sergei Rachmaninoff
Op. 3, No. 2

*Optional fingering mm. 2–11: **See introductory notes. ***See introductory notes.

* in manuscript.

Tempo I

* 𝄢 ♯♯♯ and 𝄞 ♯♯♯ in manuscript. All other editions add the fourth note.

**See introductory notes.

*See note for mm. 2–11.
**See note for mm. 47–48.

à Monsieur A. Siloti

Preludes, Op. 23

I

Sergei Rachmaninoff
Op. 23, No. 1

*See introductory notes.

II

Sergei Rachmaninoff
Op. 23, No. 2

III

Sergei Rachmaninoff
Op. 23, No. 3

Tempo di Minuetto (♩ = 66)

IV

Sergei Rachmaninoff
Op. 23, No. 4

*Play the C-sharp with the knuckle, the D with the tip of the thumb.

*See note for measure 16.

*See note for measure 16.

V

Sergei Rachmaninoff
Op. 23, No. 5

44

poco a poco accel. al Tempo I

VI

Sergei Rachmaninoff
Op. 23, No. 6

VII

Sergei Rachmaninoff
Op. 23, No. 7

VIII

Sergei Rachmaninoff
Op. 23, No. 8

Allegro vivace (♩ = 108)

IX

Sergei Rachmaninoff
Op. 23, No. 9

X

Sergei Rachmaninoff
Op. 23, No. 10

*Some editions have **p**.

ABOUT THE EDITOR

ALEXANDRE DOSSIN

Considered by Martha Argerich an "extraordinary musician" and by international critics a "phenomenon" and "a master of contrasts," Alexandre Dossin keeps active performing, recording, and teaching careers.

Born in Brazil, where he lived until he was nineteen, Dossin spent nine years studying in Moscow, Russia, before establishing residency in the United States. This background allows him to be fluent in several languages and equally comfortable in a wide range of piano repertoire.

Currently on the faculty of the University of Oregon School of Music, Dossin is a graduate from the University of Texas-Austin and the Moscow Tchaikovsky Conservatory in Russia. He studied with and was an assistant of Sergei Dorensky at the Tchaikovsky Conservatory, and William Race and Gregory Allen at UT-Austin.

A prizewinner in several international piano competitions, Dossin received the First Prize and the Special Prize at the 2003 Martha Argerich International Piano Competition in Buenos Aires, Argentina. Other awards include the Silver Medal and Second Honorable Mention in the Maria Callas Grand Prix and Third Prize and Special Prize in the Mozart International Piano Competition.

He performed numerous live recitals for public radio in Texas, Wisconsin, and Illinois, including returning engagements at the Dame Myra Hess Memorial Concert Series. Dossin has performed in over twenty countries, including international festivals in Japan, Canada, the United States, Brazil, and Argentina, on some occasions sharing the stage with Martha Argerich. He was a soloist with the Brazilian Symphony, Buenos Aires Philharmonic, Mozarteum Symphony, and São Paulo Symphony, having collaborated with renowned conductors such as Charles Dutoit, Michael Gielen, Isaac Karabtchevsky, Keith Clark, and Eleazar de Carvalho.

Dossin has CDs released by Musicians Showcase Recording (2002), Blue Griffin (*A Touch of Brazil*, 2005), and Naxos (*Verdi-Liszt Paraphrases*, 2007; *Kabalevsky Complete Sonatas and Sonatinas*, 2009; *Kabalevsky Complete Preludes*, 2009; *Russian Transcriptions*, 2012), praised in reviews by *Diapason*, *The Financial Times*, *Fanfare Magazine*, *American Record Guide*, *Clavier* and other international publications.

In the United States, Alexandre Dossin was featured as the main interview and on the cover of *Clavier* magazine and interviewed by *International Piano Magazine* (South Korea). He is an editor and recording artist for several Schirmer Performance Editions.

Dossin is a member of the Board of Directors for the American Liszt Society and the President of the Oregon Chapter of the American Liszt Society. He lives in the beautiful south hills of Eugene with his wife Maria, and children Sophia and Victor.

www.dossin.net